MW00479156

Major Lessons
From Minor Bible Characters

By
Matt Hennecke

© Guardian of Truth Foundation 2014. All Rights Reserved.
No part of this book may be reproduced in any form without written
permission from the publisher. Printed in the United States of America.

ISBN 13: 978-1-58427-3967
ISBN 10: 1-58427-3968

Guardian of Truth Foundation
CEI Bookstore
220 S. Marion St., Athens, AL 35611
1-855-49-BOOKS or 1-855-492-6657
www.CEIbooks.com

> ## A NOTE TO TEACHERS
> To assist you in teaching these lessons
> notes may be available at
> the following website:
>
> ### *www.biblemaps.com*

CONTENTS

Abraham, Moses, David, Peter, Paul, and Jesus – we're pretty familiar with the "major" characters in the Bible. We listen to sermons about them on a regular basis. We've heard their stories since we were kids. We've memorized Scripture pertaining to their lives, and can tell of their victories, their challenges, and – except for Jesus – their failures.

This workbook is not about "major" characters. It's about some "minor" characters. But one might reasonably ask who is a "minor character" in the Bible or in God's scheme of things? We all have a place in God's plan. We all are a piece of the puzzle. This holds true for the "minor" characters of the Bible. Each one of them is a part of God's plan and has an effect on others in the glorious tapestry of our God. These "minor" characters are revealed in God's Word for a reason. Together let's see if we can discover some major lessons from some "minor" Bible characters.

- Matt Hennecke

READ
Genesis 4:1-17

ABEL

The story of Cain and Abel provides a glimpse into themes prevalent throughout the Bible. These two brothers represent the two approaches men take in attempting to serve God. While the Bible only hints at the problem with Cain's sacrifice, his reaction is very revealing: Cain was angry with God when his sacrifice was rejected and probably felt slighted. His anger may have stemmed from pride. Pride exaggerates our achievements and fails to attribute our success to God. Pride is offensive to God because it seeks praise that is not due. One writer put it this way: *Cain's pride in his sacrifice attempted to take credit for God's creation. While Cain planted and tended his crops, without the soil, sun and rain, those things over which God has control, Cain's sacrifice would have been nothing.* Abel apparently understood the fruits of his labor had come from God. Thus, it would seem, Cain gave an offering to *extol himself* while Abel made a sacrifice to *exalt God*.

1. What was the work Cain and Abel did according to Genesis 4:2?

2. What did each bring as an offering to the Lord?

3. How do the *qualitative* descriptions of each offering differ (4:3-4)?

Consider the following quote from William McCaffery:

"Cain brought his best, but it wasn't God's best. It wasn't second-rate. It wasn't defective. It would have won a blue-ribbon at the county fair. He brought the best of his beautiful, delicious fruit, and he brought it as an offering to the Lord. But it was not the offering, it was not the kind of sacrifice that the Lord required. It was a bloodless offering.... In the Old Testament, to worship God you brought a sacrifice of blood – a sacrifice that pointed to the Redeemer...."

4. Do you agree with McCaffery's explanation as to why God rejected Cain's sacrifice and accepted Abel's? Was the problem with the *offering*, the *offerer*, or *both*? Make your case below, but first consider these passages: Hebrews 11:4; 1 John 3:12; and Jude 11.

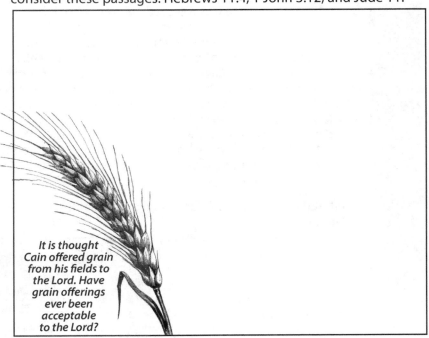

It is thought Cain offered grain from his fields to the Lord. Have grain offerings ever been acceptable to the Lord?

5. There is no biblical record of God instructing Cain or Abel in the proper way to make a sacrifice. Did God provide clear instructions? What logical conclusion about faith can we draw from Hebrews 11:4 and Romans 10:17?

6. When Cain's sacrifice was rejected, what emotion did he feel? According to the Bible what "fell" as a result of Cain's emotional state?

7. Who or what did God say was "crouching at the door"? What did he tell Cain he must do?

Major Lessons from this Minor Character

8. Hebrews 11:4 says that though Abel "is dead, he still speaks." What is Abel saying to us? Write down 2 - 3 lessons you believe we are to learn from Abel. You will be asked to share these in class.

WHAT'S IN A NAME?
In Hebrew the name Abel means "breath" or "vapor," which may add to our understanding of James' statement about the brevity of life:

...you do not know what your life will be like tomorrow. You are just a vapor that appears for a little while and then vanishes away.
- James 4:14

Excerpts from the Book of Life?

Revelation 20:12 says the following: *And I saw the dead, great and small, standing before the throne, and books were opened. Another book was opened, which is the Book of Life. The dead were judged according to what they had done as recorded in the books.* Could it be that Hebrews chapter 11 is an excerpt from the Book of Life? Of course such is mere conjecture but the idea is compelling.

By faith Abel offered to God a better sacrifice than Cain, through which he obtained

In the examples of faith given in Hebrews 11, the declaration of faith of the individuals mentioned is followed by an action taken which confirms James' point that faith without works is dead (James 2:26). Complete the chart below by considering the verses to the right of the chart:

	Individual	Action taken	
By faith	*Abel*	*offered to God a better sacrifice*	**11:4**
By faith			**11:5**
By faith			**11:7**
By faith			**11:17**
By faith			**11:24**

Now complete the following:

	Your name	Three actions you will take in the next week to demonstrate your faith:
By faith		**1.**
		2.
		3.

READ
Genesis 5:18-24

Enoch was the father of Methuselah and the great grandfather of Noah. The Bible says he walked with God after the birth of Methuselah for three hundred years (Gen. 5:22). *It was a long time for a man to support a holy life with God without any relapse worthy of notice. It is difficult for Christians to do this for a single day: how remarkable then that he should have done it for three hundred years....We have many strong characters in history. Some shine in all the brilliancy of military achievements, and are renowned for the conquest of kingdoms. Others have gathered laurels in the paths of science and illumined the world with the flashes of their genius. Others by their counsels have swayed the fate of empires. And the deeds of these have been loudly sounded by the trumpet of fame. But more is said in praise of this man of God in the few short words of our text, than is said of them all. A greater character is given him in four words, than is ascribed to the most renowned warriors and statesmen by the whole voice of history and poetry.*

Source: "Enoch Walked with God" by Edward Griffin, Puritan and Reformed Writings, http://www.puritansermons.com

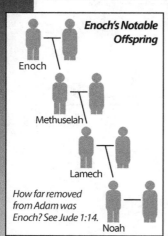

Enoch's Notable Offspring

Enoch

Methuselah

Lamech

How far removed from Adam was Enoch? See Jude 1:14.

Noah

1. The Bible says Enoch was the father of Methuselah. What else is notable about his lineage? See Luke 3:37.

2. What four or five words in our text beautifully describe the character of Enoch?

"HE WALKED WITH GOD...."

3. What does it mean to *walk* with God?

4. According to the Bible, how are we to walk?

> WALK _____ (Eph. 2:10)
>
> WALK _____ (Eph. 5:2)
>
> WALK _____ (Eph. 5:15)
>
> WALK _____ (1 Jn. 1:6-7)

5. How are we **NOT** to walk?

> DON'T WALK _____ (Jn. 11:10)
>
> DON'T WALK _____ (2 Cor. 4:2)
>
> DON'T WALK _____ (2 Cor. 5:7)
>
> DON'T WALK _____ (Psa. 1:1)

6. How can we truly *know* if we are walking with God? Is it a feeling or is there more substantial evidence?

F-3-DO
John H. Sammis, 1887

Trust And Obey
Blessed are all they that put their trust in Him. Psa. 2:12

Daniel B. Towner, 1887   F-2

1. When we walk with the Lord   In the light of His word,
2. Not a bur - den we bear,   Not a sor - row we share,
3. But we nev - er can prove   The de - lights of His love,
4. Then in fel - low - ship sweet   We will sit at His feet.

What a glo - ry He sheds on our way! While we do His good will,
But our toil He doth rich - ly re - pay; Not a grief or a loss,
Un - til all on the al - tar we lay; For the fa - vor He shows,
Or we'll walk by His side in the way; What He says, we will do;

7. Why do most people refuse to walk with God?

8. While the information about Enoch is sketchy, what other information does the Bible provide about him? See Hebrews 11:5 and Jude 1:14.

9. Most commentators agree that Enoch's walk with God began at the age of 65 (Gen. 5:21-22). If they are correct, what was the "tipping point" that caused Enoch to begin his walk with the Lord?

Major Lessons from This Minor Character ▬▬▬▬▬▬

10. Even though we have limited information about Enoch, the Holy Spirit inspired men to comment about his life. What lessons do you think we are to learn from him? Suggest some lessons to be learned below and be prepared to share them in class.

The prophet Amos revealed an important truth about what it means to walk with God when he asked, "Can two walk together, unless they are agreed?" (Amos 3:3). The word he used for "together" gives the idea of two people moving in rhythm together, as in riding a tandem bicycle. But it is not about getting God into rhythm with us; it is getting ourselves into rhythm with Him. That is what it means to walk with God.   - Greg Lauri

"BY FAITH ENOCH WAS TRANSLATED THAT HE SHOULD NOT SEE DEATH."

- Hebrews 11:5 (KJV)

In an article about Enoch, John Ritenbaugh, makes the following assertion: *The world generally interprets the statements regarding Enoch being translated (as in the KJV and other translations) to mean that Enoch was taken to heaven. That is simply untrue....the term taken away (NKJV) or translated (KJV) in Hebrews 11:5 simply means "transferred." Enoch was transferred or conveyed from one place on earth to another to escape violence aimed against him. In this other earthly place, he died like all men.* While the author of these materials disagrees, what do you think?

As you answer the question give some consideration to the following passages: Heb. 9:27; 1 Cor. 15:22. Also give some thought to whether there can there be exceptions to general biblical principles.

☐ Agree ☐ Disagree

Make your argument below:

Who else in Scripture seems to have avoided physical death – at least in the usual sense?

What is physical death according to James 2:26?

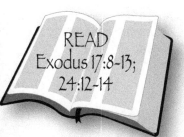

In Exodus Chapter 17 Hur is first mentioned as a companion of Moses and Aaron. From a nearby hill these three influenced the battle of God's people with the Amalekites when Hur assisted Aaron in holding up Moses' hands so God's people would prevail. Hur is mentioned again when he is left in charge with Aaron as Moses prepares to go up on Mount Sinai (Ex. 24:14). Interestingly, only Aaron is mentioned in the account of the sin God's people commit in creating and worshipping the golden calf. This has led to speculation about Hur's death. In Talmudic tradition, Hur's sudden disappearance from the Exodus narrative was the result of him being killed when he tried to prevent the making of the golden calf. The murder of Hur so intimidated Aaron, says tradition, that he complied with the demand to create the idol.

1. Why might students of the Bible tend to focus on Moses and Aaron and overlook Hur?

2. What else do we learn about Hur in the Bible?

ACCORDING TO THE HISTORIAN, JOSEPHUS, HUR WAS THE HUSBAND OF MOSES' SISTER, MIRIAM. THIS CANNOT BE VERIFIED IN SCRIPTURE.

3. Because of their age, Moses and Aaron were probably not down amongst those fighting with Joshua. What possible reasons may account for Hur not being down in the midst of the battle?

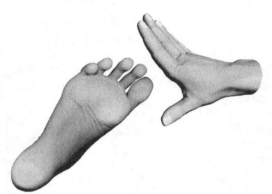

4. Relate the story of Hur to Paul's analogy in 1 Corinthians 12:14-22.

5. Indicate below others we read of in Scripture who possessed the same spirit as Hur – that is, a spirit to do what they could even though their actions might go unnoticed.

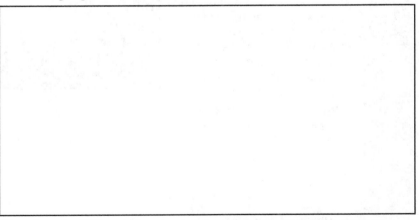

6. What does the Bible say about going unnoticed? See Matthew 6:2,5,16.

7. What might many in the Lord's church view as the "high profile" jobs or duties? What might many view as "lowly jobs" or duties?

```
┌─────── High Profile Jobs ───────┐        ┌─────── Low Profile Jobs ───────┐
│                                 │        │                                │
│                                 │        │                                │
│                                 │        │                                │
│                                 │        │                                │
└─────────────────────────────────┘        └────────────────────────────────┘
```

8. What is God's view of so-called "high profile" roles or positions? See Mark 10:35-45.

Major Lessons from This Minor Character

9. Indicate below the lessons you believe God wants us to learn from the information provided about His faithful servant Hur.

Unsung Heroes

Let us sing for unsung heroes,
  Those who lay their dreams aside.
Choosing honor more than glory
  Pledging faith with quiet pride.
Those whose uniform is courage
  yet are unashamed of tears.
Finding in their love of freedom
  power stronger than their fears.
Sing a song for unsung heroes;
  sing from sea to shining sea.
As the faithful sang before you
  sing the song of liberty.

                    - Teteana

The Spirit of Hur

Those with the spirit of Hur are found in every congregation of God's people. They are the ones who often work in the shadows. They are the ones who go largely unnoticed and unsung despite the genuine works of service they provide. Indicate below some of the "Hurs" present in this congregation and the good works they do.

Here's An Idea
Sometime in the next week, send a note of thanks or call and personally thank the "Hurs" you've identified above.

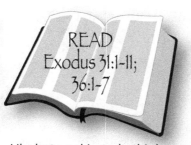

READ
Exodus 31:1-11;
36:1-7

LESSON 4

BEZALEL

Like last week's study, this lesson is about a man whose work of service and devotion was done largely in the shadows. He was not heroic – at least not in the usual sense of the word. He didn't fight any famous battles that changed the course of history. He didn't overcome any great obstacles. What he did was the special work of crafting the tabernacle and its furnishings. It is Bezalel's obscurity which makes him representative of those of us who live our lives of service to God behind the scenes. He is one of those people who, like many in the Lord's church, do work in God's kingdom without notoriety or fanfare and do so quietly and with unfailing dedication. In many ways, Bezalel's story is the story of most faithful Christians.

1. Who was Bezalel's grandfather? What inferences might be drawn about his grandfather's influence on him?

2. How did Bezalel learn of the work God intended for him? See Exodus 31:2.

3. What might we infer about Bezalel's character since he was *chosen* for this role?

Of all the tens of thousands of men of Israel, God chose Bezalel and Oholiab to craft the tabernacle and its furnishings.

4. With what was Bezalel filled (Ex. 31:3)? What does that mean?

Lampstand

5. Was Bezalel a skilled craftsman *before* he was selected by God for the special tabernacle work? Did his skill level change as a result of his "calling" (Ex. 36:1)?

The Hebrew name "Bezalel" literally means "in the shadow of God."

6. What specific elements does the Bible say Bezalel would use in building the tabernacle and its furnishings (Ex. 31:4-11)? List them below:

7. Did God give Bezalel the freedom to be creative in how he designed the tabernacle and its furnishings (Ex. 36:1-7)?

8. What was Bezalel's "heart condition" as it related to the work God gave him to do (Ex. 36:2)? Is this heart condition important in serving God? See Isaiah 29:13 and Matthew 15:8.

Laver

Major Lessons from This Minor Character

9. What lessons do you think we can learn from Bezalel? Suggest some lessons to be learned below and be prepared to share them in class.

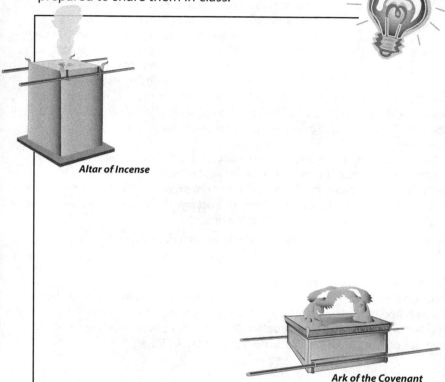

Altar of Incense

Ark of the Covenant

As a nation there is absolutely no doubt we are fixated on the heart. It is a multi-billion dollar a year effort. New equipment, new procedures, new techniques are constantly being perfected – all so we can look at and treat the heart.

To focus on the heart seems a noble endeavor, but I find myself wishing that we as a people would spend just a fraction of the time and resources looking at the heart from a different perspective – from God's perspective.   - Matt Hennecke

When God Calls

The following appeared on a religious website:

How do you know if God is calling you? First, there is an inward call. Through His Spirit, God speaks to those persons He has called to serve as pastors and ministers of His church.... Those called by God sense a growing compulsion to preach and teach the Word, and to minister to the people of God. This sense of compulsion should prompt the believer to consider whether God may be calling him to the ministry. Has God gifted you with the fervent desire to preach? Has He equipped you with the gifts necessary for ministry? Do you love God's Word and feel called to teach? That sense of urgent commission is one of the central marks of an authentic call.

Second, there is the external call. The congregation must evaluate and affirm the calling and gifts of the believer who feels called to the ministry. As a family of faith, the congregation should recognize and celebrate the gifts of ministry given to its members, and take responsibility to encourage those whom God has called to respond to that call with joy and submission.

Source: "Has God Called You? Discerning the Call to Preach" by Dr. R. Albert Mohler Jr. , AlbertMohler.com

Some Questions for Consideration

Does God "call" men and women today through the means described above? Is one called by an "inward call" or a "sense of growing compulsion"? In responding, consider 2 Thessalonians 2:14 as well as how others in the Bible were called (e.g., Moses in Exodus 3-4 and Jonah in Jonah 1).

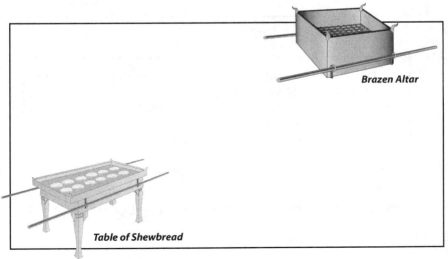

Brazen Altar

Table of Shewbread

READ
1 Samuel 25:2-38

LESSON 5

NABAL

While all of our lessons thus far have introduced us to minor biblical characters who were admirable and whose qualities we should emulate, there are also minor Bible characters whose lives were disappointing. In many cases they were men and women who were greatly blessed but who were self-centered rather than God-centered. In this lesson we will be introduced to a man whose life epitomized selfishness and foolishness. The minor character whose story offers a major lesson for us today is Nabal. He was greatly blessed with an amazing and godly wife named Abigail, and he was also blessed with considerable wealth. The problem with Nabal was he became so focused on himself, he failed to provide the honor and respect due David – God's anointed one. Before we consider Nabal, let's recall the military victories David enjoyed as God's faithful servant.

Some Background

1. What king disappointed God by his disobedience which led to the annointing of a new king? Who was to be the new king (1 Sam. 16:1-13)?

2. What impressive military victory is told in some detail in 1 Samuel 17? Who was truly behind the victory?

3. As a result of his victory, to what position was David elevated (1 Sam. 18:5)?

4. How was David viewed by the people and how did he conduct himself?

5. On the map below circle the approximate location of David's victory against Goliath and Nabal's home (1 Sam.17:1; 25:2).

6. About how many miles separate the two places?

☐ miles

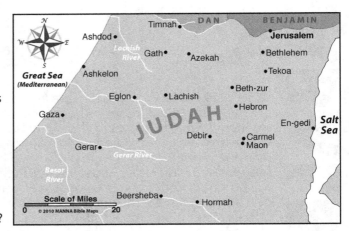

7. Were Nabal's shepherds familiar with David? How had David treated them?

8. What request did David make of Nabal?

9. What was Nabal's response to David's request (1 Sam. 25:10-11)?

10. Did Abigail know who David was and was she familiar with the work David was doing in service to the Lord? Provide evidence for your answer. See 1 Samuel 25:28.

11. Did Nabal really not know who David was, or was there a subtle message behind his words? What was he *really* saying?

12. Was David unreasonable in his reaction to Nabal's refusal for aid? Of the three characters, David, Nabal, and Abigail, who comes across as the most admirable? Why?

Major Lessons from This Minor Character

13. Nabal is by no means an admirable character, but there are lessons for us in his story. Indicate below 2-3 major lessons we should learn from this minor character:

During shearing season the sheep would be especially vulnerable as the herdsmen and workers were closely occupied with their tasks. In light of marauding Philistine bands that were stealing livestock (1 Sam. 23:5), David's protective cover was not a luxury, it was a necessity.

"Practical" Atheism

In Psalm 14:1, David writes: "The fool has said in his heart, 'There is no God.'" This passage is often quoted when we find ourselves confronting atheists or atheistic thinking, and there is no question the passage is applicable in such cases. But, to think David was writing to atheists would probably be a mistake since atheism wasn't prevalent in David's time. More prevalent was polytheism – the belief that many gods were ruling in the universe. It is more likely, then, that David was referring to those who, while knowing of the existence of a superior authority in their lives (God) acted as if He did not exist.

In our lesson about Nabal, we discover someone who clearly knew who David was but refused to submit to his authority. Nabal, by his actions, was essentially saying, "I don't need your assistance. I don't accept your rule over me. I refuse to be influenced by you!"

Atheism, then, can take two forms: it can refer to those who truly do not believe in God, but it might also refer to those who believe in God, but act as if He does not exist. This latter form of atheism might be called "practical atheism." It occurs when believers in God's existence refuse to obey His commands and refuse to accept His rule over them.

Provide some examples of those in the Bible who, while acknowledging God, did not obey him.

> Biblical examples of practical atheists:

How might *practical atheism* manifest itself in the Lord's church? In other words, how might Christians behave in ways that would for all practical purposes be saying, "There is no God"?

> Examples of how practical atheism might manifest itself in the Lord's church:

UZZAH

READ
2 Samuel 6:1-11

The Ark of the Covenant – that holy object which represented the presence of God – was captured by the Philistines nearly 20 years prior to the story involving Uzzah (1 Sam. 4-7). Having captured the Ark, the Philistines were only too willing to return it because God retaliated against

them by destroying the idol of their god Dagon and striking the inhabitants of any city where the ark was kept. Finally the Ark was returned to Israel and brought to Abinadab's house where it sat for two decades before David decided to return it to Jerusalem which lay several miles to the east. The Ark was placed on an ox cart and the journey to Jerusalem was begun. At one point the oxen pulling the cart stumbled and the Ark was about to fall. Uzzah, one of the men charged with transferring the Ark, put out his hand to prevent the Ark from falling and "the Lord's anger burned against Uzzah because of his irreverent act; therefore God struck him down and he died...." Instead of thanks for his quick action, Uzzah was executed. What lessons are we to learn from these events?

1. What instructions were given when the Ark was built regarding its transport? See Ex. 25:10-15. What were *not* to be removed?

2. Reconcile the above instructions regarding the "poles" for carrying the Ark with the instructions of Numbers 4:5-6.

3. Who were the people specifically authorized to carry the Ark? See Numbers 4:15. Why do you think God made so many restrictions regarding the Ark?

4. Who originally conceived of the idea of transporting the Ark on a cart (1 Sam. 6:7-9, 12)? Did the precedent they set influence God's people? Are similar precedents set in the religious world today that influence God's people? List a few.

5. What insight to Uzzah's death might be gotten from the following passages?

┌─ Proverbs 16:2 ─────────────────────────────────────┐
│   │
│   │
└───┘

┌─ Proverbs16:25 ─────────────────────────────────────┐
│   │
│   │
└───┘

┌─ Proverbs 21:2 ─────────────────────────────────────┐
│   │
│   │
└───┘

6. Were Uzzah's motives good? Was his heart set on doing the right thing?

7. Was God's outburst against Uzzah overly harsh? How did David feel about what happened? How do you feel about what happened?

8. Who in authority was *ultimately* responsible for moving the Ark and for allowing the violation of God's instructions (1 Chron. 13:1-14)? Why didn't he suffer for the violation of God's instructions?

Major Lessons from This Minor Character

9. Indicate below 2-3 major lessons we should learn from this minor character.

Did You Know?

The oxen stumbled on a threshing floor. A threshing floor is an area of hard packed soil used to separate grain from the chaff by oxen pulling a sled or other heavy object. For a threshing floor to work, it had to be hard and level. So at the most level, smooth part of the entire trip, the oxen stumbled! How do you account for this?

Does the End Justify the Means?

It is probably fair to assume Uzzah thought preventing the Ark from falling was a good *end*. The *means* he used to accomplish that *end* were obviously not pleasing to God. In the spaces below provide some examples of religious practices that while, perhaps intending a good *end*, often use a *means* that is not authorized or approved by God:

An unauthorized "means"	A "good" end
Reach out and touch Ark to steady it.	Keep Ark from falling.

If the *means* is wrong, can the *end* be truly "good"?

Does a "good" *end* ever justify unauthorized *means*?

The ends/means dilemma is a popular scenario in ethics discussions. The "ends justifying the means" usually involves doing something wrong to achieve a positive end and justifying the wrongdoing by pointing to a good outcome.

If it hadn't been for the terrible story of King David's sinful relationship with Bathsheba, it is quite possible we would never have heard of the character whose life we will consider in this lesson. The story of Uriah the Hittite is both one of the most troubling found in the pages of the Old Testament and one that is full of lessons for those who have truly committed themselves to the service of the Lord. In my earliest memories of the stories I was taught at home and in Bible class, this was the one I struggled with greatly. As a young boy I was enamored with David: his courageous confrontation with Goliath, his selection as King, his great and glorious victories against the Philistines. For me, David was the perfect role model. I wanted to be like him. Then, without apology, the biblical record tells us of David's wandering eye, his adultery, and his murder of one of his most devoted servants. It was years later when I was revisiting the story that I began to see in Uriah the Hittite a man who could truly serve as a role model for us all!

1. According to the Bible, how were the Hittites to be treated by God's people (Deut. 7:1-6; Ezra 9:1)?

2. How do you account for Uriah being a member of the armies of Israel?

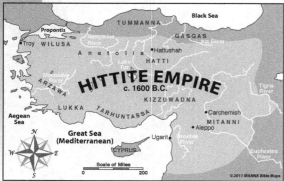

3. Many suggest Uriah was a convert to Judaism. If so, what can we infer about his character?

4. What about Uriah's character is indicated by his refusal to do the King's bidding to go home?

Did You Know?
Historians credit the Hittites with inventing iron that was used to forge weapons. They also developed siege tactics which were used by other nations. As warriors they were noted for their ferocity.

5. Upon whom was Uriah's heart set as indicated by his decision to sleep at the entrance of the palace rather than go home to his wife? Relate his devotion to Matthew 10:37-39.

Put Uriah out in front where the fighting is fiercest. Then withdraw from him so he will be struck down and die.

6. What was it about Uriah's character that gave David the confidence to have Uriah himself carry the letter containing instructions for his death?

7. While this lesson is not intended to be about David, what can we learn about the progressive nature of sin from David's actions? What contrasts can you draw between David and Uriah?

8. What is the irony of Psalm 41:9?

Major Lessons from This Minor Character

9. Indicate below 2-3 major lessons we should learn from this minor character.

In Hebrew the name Uriah means "my light is God."

Is Uriah a Type of Christ?

There is no more unlikely place to find a type of Christ than among the Hittites, yet we can't read the account of the man who was Bathsheba's husband without seeing that in him God would indeed have us see a picture of His Son. Remembering that Christ is God, in relation to whom Israel is frequently described as His adulterous wife, it isn't difficult to see here a picture of Christ and Israel. The omission of any recorded evil relative to Uriah points to the moral perfection of Christ, while the adultery of Bathsheba portrays, not only the sin of Israel, but of the whole world. All men have proved unfaithful to God. The meaning of her name ("daughter of the oath") reminds us that the nation she represents is also the daughter of the oath, for it is to Israel that God has promised every blessing. The meaning of Uriah's name is equally significant, for it means, "My light is God." It was so with Christ. God the Father was His light always, the Lord Himself being the Light of the world. David's treacherous scheming to accomplish the death of this upright man scarcely needs comment. It is clearly a foreshadowing of the treacherous scheming of the Jewish leaders to slay Christ.

Source: "Types of Christ in the Old Testament" by James Melough, online document at http://greenmeadows-stillwaters.com

Do you agree with James Melough that Uriah is a "type" of Christ?

If so, what other aspects of Uriah's story remind you of events involving Christ?

READ
Jeremiah 38:1-18

The setting for our study are the dark days just before the destruction of Jerusalem. God's people have turned from God and His wrath is about to be unleashed. The Babylonians have surrounded the city and rather than seeking God, King Zedekiah has sought help from Egypt. Isaiah declares God's displeasure in Isaiah 30:1-2:

> Woe to the rebellious children....who execute a plan but not Mine, and make an alliance but not of My Spirit, in order to add sin to sin; who proceed down to Egypt, without consulting Me, to take refuge in the safety of Pharoah, and to seek shelter in the shadow of Egypt!

Jeremiah tells the people to surrender to the Babylonian forces and their lives and the city will be spared, but if they resist they will be destroyed and the city torched (Jer. 38:2-3, 17-18).

1. How receptive were God's people to the words of Jeremiah? See Jeremiah 37:1-2.

2. What happened to Jeremiah when he was traveling to the land of Benjamin? See Jeremiah 37:11-16.

3. What was Jeremiah's prophecy recorded in Jeremiah 38:2-3?

4. What was the reaction of the King's officials to Jeremiah's prophecy (38:4-6)?

5. Why were the people so resistant to the words of Jeremiah? Relate your answer to 2 Timothy 4:3.

6. From what country was Ebed-Melech? What role or function did he play in the King's palace?

7. What did Ebed-Melech do when he heard of the fate that had befallen Jeremiah?

© 2006 MANNA
www.biblemaps.com

8. List below all the lessons we can learn from Ebed-Melech and be prepared to share them in class.

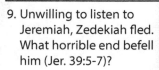

Ebed-Melech means "servant of a king," so this may have been his title and not a name.

9. Unwilling to listen to Jeremiah, Zedekiah fled. What horrible end befell him (Jer. 39:5-7)?

10. What became of Ebed-Melech (Jer. 39:15-18; James 1:12)?

SUFFERING FOR THE TRUTH

Other than Jesus Christ, list below three examples of biblical characters who suffered for preaching or teaching the truth. In the examples you cite, did anyone come to the preacher's or teacher's aid or defense?

1.

2.

3.

11. What can a Christian do in today's church to display a spirit similar to that of Ebed-Melech?

12. Describe an occasion when you were confronting difficulties and someone threw you a rope, so to speak.

13. Who in our congregation is suffering right now, and what could you do to throw them a rope?

READ
Luke 2:21-38

Anna is one of the most amazing women found in the pages of the New Testament, but there are only three short verses (Luke 2:36-38) that reveal her sterling character. By the time we meet Anna in the biblical record she is an old woman, and while it is never prudent in our culture to refer to an elderly female as an "old lady," the Bible sets tactfulness aside and in describing Anna blurts out, "she was very old" (NIV). Despite her age, or, perhaps, because of her age, Anna demonstrates many wonderful qualities that should not be over-looked in our study of minor Bible characters. In Anna we will discover attributes that should characterize all Christians and will learn that while she is certainly a "minor" character in terms of the information provided, Anna is a "major" character in teaching us how to live a life of dedicated service to the Lord.

1. What two requirements of the Law were Joseph and Mary fulfilling when they came to the Temple?

┌─ Exodus 13:2; Numbers 18:15-16 ─────────────────
│
│
└

┌─ Leviticus 12:2-4 ──────────────────────────────
│
│
└

2. What was accomplished by the paying of five, silver shekels (Num. 18:16)? What is ironic about this as it relates to the infant Jesus?

Five
shekels
of silver

3. Based on the verses above, how old was Jesus when brought to Jerusalem?

4. What inference can be made about Joseph and Mary's financial situation from the offering they brought (v. 24)?

5. List below all the specific declarations Simeon made about the infant Jesus (Luke 2:30-32, 34).

6. List below all the specific information we are told about Anna in Luke 2:36-38. Circle on the map where Anna probably was when she saw the infant Jesus.

Anna the Proclaimer

When Anna approached Joseph and Mary she immediately recognized Jesus as the Messiah, and her reaction was very telling. Like the disciples who will come after her, she is driven to bear witness to what she has seen. Mary was the first to have the good news announced to her, but Anna is the first to understand fully and proclaim the good news.

- Ben Witherington III

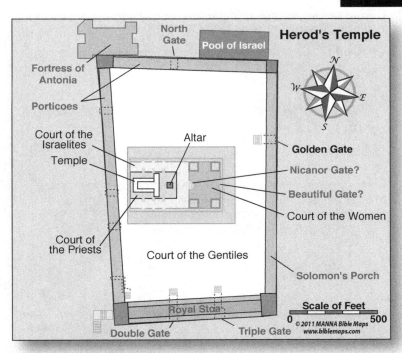

Herod's Temple

7. The Temple was a busy place with many priests engaged in Temple work. How is it that Simeon and Anna were the ones who recognized the Messiah in the infant Jesus?

Major Lessons from This Minor Character

8. Though we aren't provided with much information, there is still much to admire about Anna. What lessons for us are revealed in the life of this extraordinary woman? Be ready to share your observations.

THE PRIME OF LIFE

The world defines the "prime of life" differently from the way God does. The world sees it as that season when we are the most *physically strong* and *mentally acute*. But God sees it as that season when we are most *spiritually strong* and *intellectually humbled*. The world considers us in our prime when we have the greatest fame. The Bible reveals it as being when we most want to please God. The world defines our prime as when we are in the best position to build our own empire. Scripture defines it as when we are most focused on advancing God's Kingdom.

9. Provide three biblical examples of people who exhibited high energy and devotion to God even in their old age.

10. Who in our congregation are elderly but continue to show a high level of energy and devotion to the Lord?

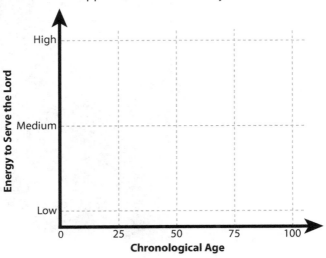

11. Plot a curve on the graph below of what *typically* happens to the level of service as Christians grow older. Next plot what *should* happen based on our study of Anna.

READ
John 17:1-19

It is difficult for us to imagine what it must have been like to live in Israel during the days of Christ. Providing adequate food, clothing, and shelter for one's family was difficult enough, but making matters worse was the fact that the Jews living in Israel were a people under Roman rule. Every day they saw evidence of the occupying Roman army. In such a context, it is understandable why many Jews sought a "warrior Messiah" – a savior who would throw off the shackles of Roman rule and lead the people to freedom. It should come as no surprise, then, that Roman soldiers were often despised because of what they represented. What is surprising, even startling, is that the New Testament record of one class of Roman soldiers – centurions – reveals them in every single instance to be admirable, even noble men. The question is why? Why are Roman centurions presented in such a positive light in the Bible?

1. Without looking ahead, list below all of the centurions you can think of mentioned in the New Testament.

The Roman Army Hierarchy

The Roman army was organized by legions, cohorts, and centuries. The one who had authority over and led a century was a "centurion."

1 legion = 10 cohorts
1 cohort = 6 centuries
1 century = 100 men

The Imperial Roman army was comprised exclusively of Roman citizens most of whom were volunteers.

CENTURION OF MATTHEW 8

What positive attributes do you see in the centurion of Matthew 8:5-13?

Request for a Servant

What statement did Jesus make about this centurion that would be shocking to the Jewish community?

CENTURION OF MATTHEW 27

What positive attributes do you see in the centurion of Matthew 27:54?

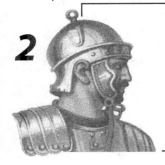

At Jesus' Crucifixion

Generate a list of attributes you think would be needed to qualify to be a centurion.

CENTURION OF ACTS 10

What positive attributes do you see in the centurion of Acts 10:1-8, 24-33?

Cornelius

How do you account for the speed with which this centurion responded to the angel's instructions?

CENTURION OF ACTS 22

What positive attributes do you see in the centurion of Acts 22:20-29?

4

An Attempted Scourging

About what did this centurion seem particularly knowledgeable?

CENTURIONS OF ACTS 23

What positive attributes do you see in the centurions of Acts 23:12-24, 31?

5

An Attempted Assassination

Consider all of the centurions mentioned in the above passage as you list the positive attributes.

CENTURION OF ACTS 27

What positive attributes do you see in the centurion of Acts 27:1-11, 41-44?

6

Julius

Why do you think this centurion was so protective of the prisoner over which he had responsibility?

9. As you review the attributes of all the centurions, what are the *common* attributes they share that make them admirable? What, perhaps, is the single common and most important attribute?

Major Lessons from These Minor Characters

10. What lessons can we learn from these men? Indicate your answers in the space below and be prepared to share your observations.

For Discussion

In Matthew 8:8-10 what connection is made between Jesus' authority and the centurion's faith? Who is the "Word" according to John 1:1,14?

In the beginning was the Word, and the Word was with God, and the Word was God. He was in the beginning with God. All things came into being through Him, and apart from Him nothing came into being that has come into being. In Him was life, and the life was the Light of men. The Light shines in the darkness, and the darkness did not comprehend it. There came a man sent from God, whose name was John. He came as a witness, to testify about the Light, so that all might believe through him. He was not the Light, but he came to testify about the Light. There was the true Light which, coming into the world, enlightens every man. He was in the world, and the world was made through Him, and the world did not know Him. He came to His own, and those who were His own did not receive Him. But as many as received Him, to them He gave the right to become children of God, even to those who believe in His name, who were born, not of blood nor of the will of the flesh, nor of the will of man, but of God. And the Word became flesh, and dwelt among us, and we saw His glory, glory as of the only begotten from the Father, full of grace and truth. - John 1:1-14

READ
Luke 19:1-9

ZACCHEUS

11 LESSON

Life is full of obstacles – those things that come between where you are and where you want to be (or should be). The dictionary defines an obstacle as "something that stands in the way or opposes." That seems an appropriate definition especially in things spiritual. Why? Because there is a Deceiver who stands and opposes us in our efforts to seek and find salvation in Jesus Christ. In this lesson we will look at a fairly obscure character – though he is widely known because of a childrens' song. There were many obstacles in Zaccheus' way, but in the few short verses devoted to him we see him successfully overcome them because of a good heart and divine guidance. Many of us, like Zaccheus, have obstacles that we must overcome. Perhaps, by studying this man we can find insight in how to do just that.

1. What was Zaccheus' profession?

"Zaccheus" from the Greek form of the Hebrew "Zakkay" means "pure, innocent, or righteous."

2. In the minds of the people of Zaccheus' day, what sins were associated with tax collectors? See Matt. 11:19 and Luke 18:11.

3. What is ironic about the meaning of Zaccheus' name and the profession he chose for himself?

6 Obstacles in Zaccheus' Way. . . and Potentially in Our Way Too

1.

Relate the obstacle to the following verses:
Exodus 23:2; Matthew 7:13-14

How might this obstacle prevent us from seeking the Lord?

2.

Relate the obstacle to the following verses:
Matthew 19:16-24; 1 Timothy 6:10

How might this obstacle prevent us from seeking the Lord?

3.

Relate the obstacle to the following verses:
Matthew 5:29-30

How might this obstacle prevent us from seeking the Lord?

4.

Relate the obstacle to the following verses:
Luke 3:12-13

How might this obstacle prevent us from seeking the Lord?

5.

Relate the obstacle to the following verses:
Philippians 3:13-15

How might this obstacle prevent us from seeking the Lord?

6.

Relate the obstacle to the following verses:
1 John 1:8-10

How might this obstacle prevent us from seeking the Lord?

Major Lessons from This Minor Character

4. What lessons can we learn from Zaccheus? Indicate your ideas in the space below and be prepared to share your observations.

The Blame Game

At what game do you excel? Football? Basketball? Tennis? Perhaps your skills lie in the playing of some board game. Sadly, many people have perfected another game. What game is that? The "blame game" – the ability to blame other people or other things for our failings, flaws, and sins. In recent years the "blame game" has developed a new wrinkle: people have begun blaming biology for their sins. The most glaring example of this effort to excuse sin because of biology comes from the scientific community and the increasing number of studies that claim homosexuality is a matter of genetics. The conclusion reached by many who embrace such studies is that practicing homosexuality can't be wrong if it's due to one's genetic predisposition.

- What notable Bible character attempted to excuse his responsibility because of a biological limitation? See Exodus 4:10-17.

- What was God's response to his attempted excuse?

- What notable biblical character did not let a biological limitation prevent him from his duty and service to God (2 Cor. 12:7-10)?

DNA molecule

- What biological excuse could Zaccheus have used to keep from seeking the Lord?

- From the above examples what can we conclude about using our biological makeup as an excuse for sin? See Romans 8:5-8.

*Zacchaeus was a wee little man,
and a wee little man was he.
He climbed up in a sycamore tree,
the Savior for to see.*

*And as the Savior passed that way,
he looked up in the tree,
And said, "Zaccheus you come down
For I'm going to your house with thee."*

The Bible reveals that when Jesus Christ was crucified and died on the cross many unusual things occurred: the sun was obscured, the veil of the temple was torn in two, the earth shook, rocks were split, tombs were opened, and many bodies were raised (Matt. 27:45, 51-53). As amazing as those events were, another strange thing happened: two members of the Sanhedrin – the supreme court of ancient Israel – openly and unashamedly took Jesus's body, wrapped it in a clean linen cloth, and laid it in a new tomb. One of those men, Joseph of Arimathea, is the subject of this

lesson. The Bible, as with the other characters we have studied, does not provide much information about Joseph, but it is interesting that all four gospels mention him and the action he took on that sad day when the Son of God was crucified. What can we learn from this obscure man?

1. Circle the city of Joseph's origin on the map. About how far is the city from Jerusalem?

2. What is the first reference to Joseph found in the Bible?

3. How many years *before* Jesus was crucified was the reference made about Joseph?

4. What details are given about Joseph in Matthew 27:57-61? List them below.

5. What additional details do we learn about Joseph in Mark 15:43-47?

6. What is meant by the statement that Joseph was "waiting for the kingdom"?

The Sanhedrin

Sanhedrin comes from the Greek term *sunedrion* (literally, "sitting together") meaning council. The Sanhedrin was both a Jewish judicial and administrative body. The Sanhedrin was comprised of 71 members – including the high-priestly family, scribes, and lay elders. It operated under Roman oversight with respect to its taxing, law enforcement, and other administrative functions. When Jesus was brought before the Sanhedrin, Caiaphas presided. Some believe Moses, at the Lord's instruction, founded the Sanhedrin (Num. 11:16-17).

7. What additional details do we learn of Joseph in Luke 23:50-53?

8. Did Joseph consent with the other members of the Sanhedrin to the plan and action they had taken in regard to Jesus? Reconcile your answer with Mark 14:64.

9. What additional details do we learn about Joseph in John 19:38-40?

10. Who joined Joseph in taking and preparing the body of Jesus for burial?

11. List below all the things you can think of that Joseph might have lost had he been open about his discipleship.

12. So why now? Why did Joseph *choose this moment* to reveal himself as a disciple of Jesus? After all, Jesus is dead! What possible benefit could come from declaring himself now?

Major Lessons from This Minor Character

13. What lessons can we learn from Joseph? Indicate the lessons you've learned and be ready to share them.

Did You Know?
Though it cannot be confirmed scripturally, the Jewish Talmud records that Joseph was the great-uncle of Jesus, a younger brother of Mary's father.

SECRET DISCIPLESHIP

Shhhhhhh! Can you keep a secret? For many Christians keeping secret the fact that they believe in Jesus Christ has become a manner of life. The same fear that kept Joseph from being open about his discipleship afflicts us some 2,000 years later. Even Peter, the apostle, tried to hide his belief in Jesus (Matt. 26:69-75). What are the reasons many true believers in our times are fearful of revealing their faith? List below 2-3 reasons Christians might hide their discipleship.

1.

2.

3.

14. How can we be more bold in our service to the Lord? How can we, like Joseph of Arimathea, overcome our fear and declare our faith in Jesus Christ?

*What does Revelation 21:8
say about the fearful or cowardly?*

READ
2 Timothy 4:6-10

DEMAS

Whenever I drive past a cemetery I can't help but wonder about the lives of the people whose bodies are buried there. On most tombstones are both the year of birth and death, and between those two years is a dash. It was the "dash" that became the subject of a poem entitled *The Dash Between* written by Danny Richard Hahlbohm. The poem recounts a man who was speaking at a friend's funeral. The main point of the poem, beautifully expressed, was that the birthdate and the deathdate mattered little. What truly mattered was the dash between the years. Why? Because that little dash represented the time of living. Right now, as you read this, your birthdate is known, but your deathdate is not. More important is how you are spending the years in between. In other words, what are you doing with the "dash"?

As best it can be determined, Demas, who is the subject of this lesson, lived from 50 to 67 A.D. You may be asking, "Wait a minute, was Demas really only 17 years old?" Let's study the three verses which speak of Demas and see what lessons we can learn from a man who only lived *spiritually* for about 17 years.

1. What do we learn about Demas in Colossians 4:14?

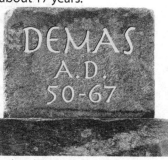

2. What do we learn about Demas in Philemon 1:23-24?

3. Do some research. Approximately when were each of the following Pauline epistles written?

TO THE SAINTS AND FAITHFUL BRETHREN IN CHRIST WHO ARE AT COLOSSAE...

Colossians | Was written approx. A.D. _____

Philemon | Was written approx. A.D. _____

2 Timothy | Was written approx. A.D. _____

4. According to John 3:3, what did Jesus say one had to do to see the kingdom of God?

5. If Demas heard and obeyed the gospel while Paul was on his second missionary journey, then when was Demas "born" again?

Possible Date of Spiritual Birth

Paul's 2nd Journey A.D. 49-52
Outbound - - - - -
Return ▪ ▪ ▪ ▪

MACEDONIA • Philippi
Berea • Thessalonica
Troas
BITHYNIA
GALATIA
Aegean Sea
ACHAIA
Thyatira
ASIA
CAPPADOCIA
Corinth • • Athens
Ephesus
Antioch ▽
PISIDIA • Iconium
Miletus Colossae Lystra
Attalia Derbe
LYCIA CILICIA
Tarsus Antioch
Seleucia •
SYRIA
Rhodes
Cyprus • Salamis
Paphos •
Great Sea (Mediterranean)
Tyre
Caesarea
Jerusalem

Some believe the city Demas went to (2 Tim. 4:10) was his home town and the city where he was converted by Paul on his second missionary journey.

Scale of Miles
0   200

6. When did Demas "die spiritually" as indicated by his forsaking Paul because he "loved the present world"? Hint: When was 2 Timothy written?

Possible Date of Spiritual Death

7. About what do the following passages warn? What conclusions can we draw about Demas if he abandoned the faith?

James 4:4

1 John 2:15

8. What three primary enticements exist in the world (1 John 2:16)?

9. If, as most scholars agree, Demas abandoned the faith, what impact do you think his action had on the following?
   • The early church?

   • On the apostle Paul (Phil. 3:18)?

   • On his own eternal future (Matt. 16:26)?

Major Lessons from This Minor Character

10. What lessons do you think we can learn from Demas? Suggest some lessons to be learned below and be prepared to share them in class.

Whoever wants to be a friend of the world makes himself an enemy of God.

THE LONELY EMBER

A member of a certain church, who previously had been attending services regularly, stopped going. After a few weeks, the preacher decided to visit him. It was a chilly evening. The preacher found the man at home alone, sitting before a blazing fire.

Guessing the reason for the preacher's visit, the man welcomed him, led him to a big chair near the fireplace and waited. The preacher made himself comfortable but said nothing. In the grave silence, he contemplated the play of the flames around the burning logs.

After some minutes, the preacher took the fire tongs, carefully picked up a brightly burning ember and placed it to one side of the hearth all alone. Then he sat back in his chair, still silent. The host watched all this in quiet fascination. As the one lone ember's flame diminished, there was a momentary glow and then its fire was no more. Soon it was cold and "dead as a doornail."

Not a word had been spoken since the initial greeting.

Just before the preacher was ready to leave, he picked up the cold, dead ember and placed it back in the middle of the fire. Immediately it began to glow once more with the light and warmth of the burning coals around it.

As the preacher reached the door to leave, his host said, "Thank you so much for your visit and especially for the fiery sermon. I shall be back in church next Sunday."

Some Things to Think About: Assessing Your Spiritual Health

11. When were you "spiritually" born?

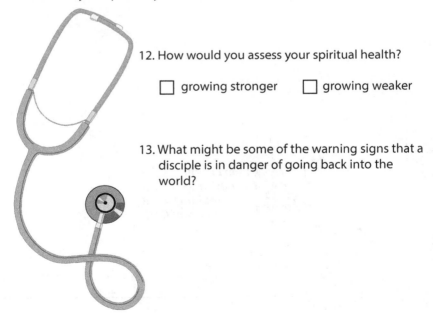

12. How would you assess your spiritual health?

☐ growing stronger ☐ growing weaker

13. What might be some of the warning signs that a disciple is in danger of going back into the world?